BY GOD, I WILL
The Biblical Covenants

BY GOD, I WILL

The Biblical Covenants

David Pawson

Anchor Recordings

First published in 2013
by Anchor Recordings Ltd
72 The Street, Kennington, Ashford TN24 9HS UK

www.davidpawson.org

ISBN 978-0-9569376-8-1

Printed In Great Britain by Imprint Digital, Exeter

Contents

This book is based on a series of talks. Originating as it does from the spoken word, its style will be found by many readers to be somewhat different from my usual written style. It is hoped that this will not detract from the substance of the biblical teaching found here.

As always, I ask the reader to compare everything I say or write with what is written in the Bible and, if at any point a conflict is found, always to rely upon the clear teaching of scripture.

David Pawson

Foreword

"I swear by Almighty God that the evidence I give will be the truth, the whole truth and nothing but the truth."[1] Anyone who has attended a court case will be familiar with this formula, but what does it mean?

It is the vestigial remains of an era when most people took God seriously. It was intended to put the fear of God into a witness, by reminding them that he can and will severely punish all liars and particularly those who swear an oath not to do so. It is to call on a higher and greater power than one's self to destroy anyone who breaks such a vow made in his presence. It was meant to be a most solemn moment in a trial.

The words are said with one hand holding a Bible, for two reasons. First, it identified which God was being called on as a witness, namely the God of the Jews (including Jesus). Scripture makes abundantly clear how he will deal with disregarded vows made 'before' him, and he is present everywhere so hears every word (Deuteronomy 23:21).

The classic example is that of Jephthah in Judges 11.

Asking the Lord to give him victory over the Ammonites, he foolishly vowed that whatever came out to meet him as a returning victor he would sacrifice *it* (clearly expecting an animal, perhaps a pet), in gratitude for answered prayer. But it turned out to be a *she*, his own and only daughter. She, fearing God's wrath against her father, willingly gave up her life and with it, any hope of marriage. It is one of the most sobering stories in the Bible and a solemn reminder that vows made in God's hearing must be kept.

But times have changed. The wrath of God is no longer considered to be a threat. People fear neither God nor hell, or even believe in either. 'Swearing' has been reduced to careless blasphemies and obscenities contaminating the two most sacred relationships known to us ('hell' and 'fuck' are the most common examples; even 'bloody' is a contraction of 'by Our Lady', i.e. Mary).

So swearing 'by God' has almost died out, except in the courts, where it has become a trivial ritual, tradition rather than truth. Many holding the Bible have never opened and read it. The nearest they get to such an oath is the surprised expletive: 'Oh my God", whatever that means. So why is 'By God' the first half of the title of a book about Biblical Covenants? Simply because God swears, especially when making important covenants (as with Abraham). However, there is no-one higher, bigger or stronger than himself to swear by and hold him to his oath. For God to swear 'by God' would sound very odd, almost a tautology (unnecessary repetition, as in 'reverse backwards'). Instead, he swears 'by myself'. This is even more serious, not less. God is declaring that he will destroy himself before breaking his promise. The thought of divine suicide should shock us into realising how deadly serious he is.

Which brings me to the second part of my title: 'I will'. This is a reminder that at the heart of every covenant lies a promise or, in some cases, a number of promises, always beginning with these two small words. They run right through the Bible, usually spoken by God and underlining his amazing grace in making solemn promises to his creatures.

I would be surprised if this phrase did not bring back memories of weddings to my readers, either their own or other people's. God sees all marriages as covenants, whether 'solemnised' (what a significant word!) in a church building, Register Office or anywhere else. He witnesses all marriage vows, since he is always present. This is why he hates divorce (Malachi 2:16) and why Jesus said remarriage after divorce is continual adultery (Luke 16:18). There has been the same devaluation of wedding promises as with swearing. Marriage has changed from a covenant to a mere contract. If one party reneges on their obligations the other is considered free to look elsewhere. 'Till death us do part' became the title of a TV 'sitcom' (situation comedy). The ring (a symbol of *endless* love) can be taken off as easily as it was put on. Vows made sincerely at the wedding need not be considered binding for life, especially when things become worse rather than better, poorer rather than richer, sick rather than healthy.

But when God says 'I will' he means it, absolutely. However, as we shall see, sometimes his covenants are conditional on a responding commitment from us – 'we will' (Exodus 19:8). The covenant is not then cancelled when we break it but his blessings are replaced by his curses (Deuteronomy 28).

So that explains my short, sharp title. Now read on.

Note

My editor is anxious that I should remind readers that there is a history of Christians who have refused to take any oath at all, even in a court of justice. They have taken seriously our Lord's prohibition of all swearing (Matthew 5:33–37). He was also aware that Jews in his day thought they could evade divine retribution for broken oaths by swearing by something greater than themselves (heaven, earth, Jerusalem), thus avoiding the name of God himself. For Jesus, however, these were all connected with God, who takes such oaths equally seriously. He then told his disciples that integrity and reliability of speech should be all that is necessary. Attempts to assure truthfulness with any additional words is from the devil, the 'father of lies' (would this include even the word 'honestly'?).

Christians today need not fear imprisonment for refusing to swear on a Bible in court. They have the option of making a 'solemn affirmation' to tell the truth. But even that goes beyond our Lord's counsel to let our 'yes' be yes and our 'no' be no.

I only used the current practice in court to illustrate swearing 'by God', not to approve the practice. But there are some things we should not do which our holy God can and does do. And swearing by God (himself) is one of them.

1

What is a Covenant?

Have you ever wondered why many churches baptise babies, some baptise children and others baptise only adults? Have you ever wondered why some churches teach you to 'tithe' your income (giving a tenth of your money to the church) while others rely on voluntary giving? Have you ever wondered why some churches worship on a Sunday and others on a Saturday, or even a Friday evening? Have you wondered why some churches have priests, altars, incense, and candles, and others don't? Have you ever wondered why some churches marry divorcees and others refuse to do so? Have you ever wondered why some churches support Israel and others don't?

Yet all these churches use the same Bible and claim to put it into practice — very puzzling, isn't it? We have to find some way through this variety of opinion and try to discover the truth. It all boils down to an understanding of the Bible.

What single word will unlock the whole Bible? There are two candidates for that key word. One is "kingdom", but that word, although it runs through the Bible, changes its meaning. In the Old Testament it is the kingdom of Israel and in the New Testament it is the kingdom of God (or kingdom of heaven). But I want to present you with another word, which I believe is the key both to sorting out all those issues I mentioned and to unlocking the whole Bible: the word "covenant".

In this book we ask two vital questions: how many covenants are there in the Bible, and how many of them apply to me as a Christian? It is because there are different answers to those questions that we have such varieties of church teaching.

When we ask how many covenants there are, some people say there is only one in the whole Bible and they call it "the covenant of grace", though that particular phrase cannot be found anywhere in scripture.

Then there are those who say there are only two covenants in the Bible: the Old and the New. Then there are those who say there are three, there are those who say there are five, and there are those who say there are seven. Isn't it confusing? When you get more than one covenant in the Bible, how many of those affect Christians? How many of those link us to God?

What is a covenant? It is a binding agreement

between parties or two persons – a very solemn agreement carrying mutual obligations between the two, based on promises, based on commitment. We don't have many examples of covenants in daily life and therefore it is not a word we tend to use in ordinary society. The word we do use for a binding agreement is "contract" and life is full of contracts – business contracts particularly. But I want to show you that there is a huge difference between a covenant and a contract. You can never have a contract with God, but you would be amazed how many people try to get into an agreement with him that is something like a contract – "I'll do this if you do that". A covenant is very different. We begin by thinking about contracts because we are more familiar with them.

If I want to get a house built, I look around for a builder, a contractor. We would work out the terms of the contract between us because we are on equal terms. That is the key to a contract: each party has something that the other person needs, so you are in a position to bargain. The builder has skill, labour and materials, and you have money. He wants your money and you want his skill, materials and labour. So you negotiate, and you are both in a position to drive a hard bargain. You agree and sign a contract with the builder that he will build the house for a certain price and in a certain time. It is a serious and binding thing.

If one party fails to keep his promise, the other party may be released from the contract or may sue for compensation.

Of course there are many kinds of contracts. I have cited a simple building contract but business is built on contracts all over the world, all day and every day.

Another kind of contract is a peace treaty or a ceasefire or an armistice when there has been a war, and that again is agreed by two parties, both of whom are in a position to negotiate. You make a contract for peace.

What about a covenant? How is it different? If I can put it this way, a contract is bilateral – two equal parties are in a position to negotiate the terms; each has something the other wants – whereas a covenant is unilateral, one-sided. *It is agreed by one party who settles the terms, because they are in a stronger position*. The only thing the other party can do is to accept the covenant or reject it, they cannot change it. Furthermore, in a covenant if one party lets the covenant down that does not release the other party from the promises that are made *provided the covenant has been unconditional*. Covenants can be conditional but normally they are unconditional. Once they are accepted they are binding, but even if they are broken by the weaker party, the stronger is still bound to keep the promises made, *if* it is an unconditional covenant.

So when we come across a covenant in the Bible the first question you ask is this: "Is it conditional or unconditional?" If it is conditional it is more like a contract, but if it is unconditional it binds the party who makes it, whatever happens on the other side— and that is quite a big difference from a contract. I sometimes ask people the question, "Do you think marriage is a contract or a covenant?" Christians are aware that God intended marriage to be a covenant. But in our society it is rapidly becoming a contract, an agreement between two equal parties who negotiate with each other, and each has something the other wants. I am afraid most marriages today are contracts, which is why so many break up. "As long as I love you or you love me we're married, but if you stop loving me, or I stop loving you, the contract is finished." One feature of modern life which is incredible to me is called a "prenuptial contract" or a "prenuptial agreement" as to what you will do with the property or the money if you get a divorce. Fancy agreeing before you get married as to what you will do when you get divorced! So we are getting right away from God's understanding of marriage as a covenant and right into marriage as a contract, and that is not going to hold together.

I read about a man in the north of England whose

wife, shortly after their marriage, became unfaithful to him, started playing around with other men, becoming more and more unfaithful, and finally she left him. She was soon on the streets and rapidly went from bad to worse. His friends said, "Why don't you get a divorce? She's no good to you, you are having to look after the children yourself. Get a divorce and find a decent woman who will be faithful to you and look after your kids, and you can be a real family."

He turned on them, saying, "Never speak to me like that about my wife. She's my wife and I will love her as long as there's breath in her body." He did just that, and when, some years later, she was dying as the result of her bad living, he was at her bedside, loving her and praying for her. That is *covenant marriage*. In *contract marriag*e he would long since have given up and changed partners.

Sadly, we are in a situation where even Bible-believing Christians are treating marriage like a contract and switching partners. But we are not in a contract, God calls marriage a covenant, and even if one side breaks the terms in a covenant, the other side stays faithful to promises. See how relevant it is to talk about covenants and contracts. Historically, marriage was never an agreement between two equal partners. For better or worse, the husband was the stronger partner and that is why he proposed. Still today it is the custom that men take the initiative and 'propose' marriage.

Furthermore, traditionally (and still at many weddings) the bride's father gives her away. Usually the bride takes the husband's name, for he is the stronger of the two. He is the leader so in marriages today there are still traces of the covenant marriage. But the vast majority of marriages in the Western world are contracts. I am encouraged that one thing the economic recession doing is cutting down divorces. People can't afford to divorce now. I am almost tempted to shout "Hallelujah"!

I have been using marriage as an illustration, but I am afraid that nowadays marriage is not the best example of a covenant, so let's think of something else that is, in which I hope you are involved. Have you made your will? It is called a "last will and testament" and the word "testament" has the same meaning as "covenant."

The two parts of your Bible are called the Old Testament and the New Testament, which means the old covenant and the new covenant, but I am going to show you those are very confusing titles.

When you write your will, that is making a covenant. You are the stronger party. You have the money or property to leave to someone else. It is your voluntary will to bind yourself to give that property or money to another person. There is no negotiation (or there shouldn't be) with your relatives or friends to whom you are leaving things. You are setting the terms, you decide. You can change your will with a codicil after it has been made, right up to the day you die, but it is you who settles the terms.

A legatee can either accept what you leave them or reject it. But they cannot change your will. It is your decision. As the stronger party, you have made a covenant – a testament – to leave money or give property to other people when you are dead.

It is an interesting point, because the letter to the Hebrews in the New Testament says that when Jesus made the new covenant in his blood it could not become effective until he had died. Isn't that interesting? Your testament, covenant (or will) will not become effective until you die. Blood is associated with covenants in scripture. Death is associated with covenants in the Bible, but I am jumping ahead.

So let me now make two very important points. *Our God is a covenant-making God*. It is remarkable when you think about it that the God who made the entire universe should bind himself voluntarily to human beings. After all, he is the strong one. We are the weak ones. We are just his creatures, tiny little beings on a little speck of interstellar dust hurtling through space –

and here we are, God has voluntarily put himself under obligation to us. He need not have done it, and it is astonishing that he did, but that is what he has done. The Bible is the story of the covenants he has voluntarily made towards human beings, towards *us*. That should leave us breathless with amazement. Why should he do that? No reason at all! He could have made us, left us to go on our way – but far from it.

He has bound himself to do certain things for human beings; he has made his testament. He wants to make us his heirs. He wants to make a will in our favour. This is almost unbelievable: that God should make covenants with us, and that he should therefore *marry* human beings—which is even more startling in a sense. For him a marriage is always a covenant, and the first people he married (or made a covenant with) were Abraham, Isaac and Jacob. The amazing thing is that although he was the husband and they were the wife (as it were) of the marriage, he took their name and for ever after has been known as "the God of Abraham, Isaac, and Jacob" – a grandfather, father, and son. Their names are now written into God, they are his name. It is as though the bridegroom took the bride's name. It is extraordinary, unheard of until recently. Then he made a covenant with Israel. He says, "I married you at Sinai, you're my wife," and therefore he took the name

"Israel", and God will forever be called "the holy one of Israel" — amazing!

When Israel broke that covenant, what would God say?

God said to the prophet Hosea, "Go out and find a prostitute."

"But I'm a preacher, Lord."

"Go and find a prostitute and marry her."

"Oh," he said, "I can't do that. Think of the headlines. 'Prostitute marries preacher', or 'preacher marries prostitute'. What then?"

But God said, "Then you must have some children. I had better warn you, not all the children will be yours."

"What then, Lord"

"Well then she's going to go back on the streets, back to her old trade."

"What do I do then with the three kids?"

"Well then, Hosea, I want you to go and find her, pay the pimp who's running her and bring her back home. Put her under discipline for a time and then take her back as your wife."

"Why do I have to do all that, Lord?"

"Because that's what Israel is doing to me and that's how I feel about her, and you won't be able to convey my feelings to Israel unless you go through them yourself, so that's why."

What an incredible story. You can read all about it

in the book of Hosea.

So God married people. He entered into a covenant marriage with Israel, with Abraham, Isaac, and Jacob. He made his testament, his will, in their favour. One of the things he gave to them and left to them was the land in the Middle East which we call the Promised Land. All that was involved in his covenant with them.

So God is a God who *makes* covenants, and the second point I want to make is that **God is a God who keeps covenants.** If God ever makes a promise, he will never break it. You will find these two words all the way through the Bible: "I will." They are on God's lips almost every time. That is his will and testament – his promises to people.

Once, I took a sheet of paper and began to write down what Almighty God *cannot* do. Very quickly I had a list. It began: he cannot break a promise; he cannot tell a lie; he cannot tell a dirty joke – and I went on writing these things down until I got to thirty-one. I made it into a sermon: *The things God cannot do.* When I looked at the list I thought, "I've done all those things," but that didn't make me feel bigger than God, it made me feel very small that I can do all those things that God cannot do.

That is because of God's character—there are things that are so distasteful, so disgusting to him, and such an "abomination" to him that he cannot bring himself to do them. We need to understand what God is like. Whether or not people say they believe in God, it is what *kind* of God we do or don't believe in that really matters. For some years I was a chaplain in the Royal Air Force. When men arrived at the RAF station they had to report to the chaplains, and there were three of us on every station: Roman Catholic, Church of England, and then the "other denominations" (that was me), known as "ODs" or "odd-bods". What would happen was a couple of hundred new recruits would arrive at the station. The Church of England chaplain, representing the established church, said, "Everybody who's been christened as a baby in the Church of England come with me." He usually got three-quarters of them. Then the Roman Catholic chaplain had some ten percent. I got everyone else: Presbyterians, Methodists, Baptists, Salvation Army, Buddhists, Hindus, Muslims, agnostics and atheists.

So I was left with such a muddle and I had to look after all of them. I really enjoyed being a chaplain to atheists. An atheist would arrive, and on his card under the heading "religion" it would say "atheist". I would welcome him warmly and say, "Congratulations on your faith. You must have more faith than I have to believe that all this happened by chance and came about without any help from anyone. I just don't have enough faith to believe that. I have to believe somebody had a hand in it — much simpler. But you must be a person of great faith, congratulations."

The second thing I said to them was, "If you're killed I will have to bury you. I want to make you a solemn promise that I will not read from the Bible, that I will not say a prayer, that I will not sing a hymn, that I will not mention God. I will simply say, 'This man is dead and gone.'"

A lot of pilots were being killed at that time and I found that many people were quite happy to live as an atheist but not so happy to die as one. There is an element of risk in that, and they didn't seem very happy about my proposal for their funeral.

The third thing I would say to an atheist was, "Now sit down there and tell me what kind of God you don't believe in." After he had finished I could always say, "Well you just made me an atheist because I don't believe in that kind of God either." Always ask what kind of God they don't believe in.

I believe in a God who is *righteous*, and that means there are many things he *cannot* do. It doesn't make him weak, but it makes him a wonderful God to know. First, it means a righteous God cannot do anything wrong. He cannot do anything unfair, he cannot do anything unjust. To know that the God in charge of the universe is like that is a tremendous comfort. It also means that everything he does is right. That does not mean that everything which happens is right, but that everything *he* does, everything he is responsible for, is absolutely right.

As a pastor, one of the acute situations I had to deal with was when parents had lost a baby. It is always a shock and a sad business. The question asked again and again was, "What has God done with my baby now? Is he or she in heaven – or where? I had to be honest and say, "I don't know what God has done with your baby. The Bible doesn't answer that question. God must have a good reason for not telling us." I know that many pastors say, "Your baby is in heaven," but I can't say that because I can only affirm what the Bible says.

Although I had to say, "I don't know," I added, "If you knew God as well as I do, you would know that whatever he's done with your baby is right and you can trust him." But you have to believe in a certain kind of God to talk that way – a God who will always do right, and therefore whether he tells you or doesn't tell you what he's doing, you know and are sure that what he has done is right. This gives you a security in your soul even though it doesn't answer all your questions.

God is not only a covenant-*making* God, he is a

covenant *keeping* God. You can guarantee that **what he promises will always be**. To jump ahead for one moment, that is why I am quite sure that the Promised Land still belongs to the descendants of Abraham – because God promised it to them. That is the biggest factor in the whole Middle East political situation, though the politicians are ignoring it. But God has not gone back on his promise. It is the Promised Land and always will be. That shows how important the covenants are – all the more amazing because God keeps his promises.

He is reliable; he is faithful. You can trust him right to the end. You know that he will keep his word.

Now for my answer to the question, "How many covenants are there?" There are *five*. When the question is asked, "And how many affect me as a Christian?" the answer is *four*. There is one covenant that doesn't. There is one that is exclusively Jewish – it is for the Jews but not for me. It is amazing how people can get confused and put people back under the covenant that doesn't belong to Christians.

2

The Five Covenants

We have seen that a covenant is unilateral: one person decides the terms, one person puts himself under obligation to another and makes certain promises. The other person cannot change the terms. The only choice they have is either to accept or reject — and that is a covenant. God only makes covenants with people; he doesn't make contracts.

Nevertheless, many people do try to make a contract with God. I remember a churchgoer saying, "I was in World War Two in the thick of a battle. Bullets were flying, shells were exploding, people were dying around me, and I said to God, 'If you will get me back safely to my family, I'll go to church every Sunday.'" That was a contract and he didn't keep his part of it.

He asked me, "Can you have a second bite at the cherry, or a second chance?"

I replied, "Yes you can, but not on that basis. You can't make a bargain with God."

There is a very simple reason you cannot have a

contract with God, which is that you have nothing that he wants or needs. One of my favourite texts is in Psalm 50, in which God says, *"If I were hungry I wouldn't tell you."* I love that text but I have never heard anyone preach on it. You probably know the next verse, *"The silver and the gold are mine, and the cattle on a thousand hills."*

God's words mean: *Everything that you've got is already mine* —and it is. All the wealth in the world belongs to God, even if we think it belongs to us. He can give it and take it away, just like that.

So it is amazing how many people try to make a bargain with God as if they are in a position to do so. Jacob was a classic case. Do you remember when he dreamt about the ladder reaching to heaven, the night he had run away from home? He fled from his brother Esau whom he had cheated, and he was homesick already.

Jacob said to God, "If you get me back to my father's house safely, I'll give you a tenth of all I get" —a tithe. That did not establish his relationship with God because you cannot bargain with God like that. Years later, Jacob was on his way home again and rather dreading meeting his brother Esau. He was so scared, he wanted God to bless him, and the night before he met Esau he wrestled with God, saying, "I will not let you go until you bless me" —still trying to bargain. God had to break that man, and he dislocated his hip. From then on, Jacob walked with a limp. He was a broken man, but now God could use him.

Now he realised his weakness, he wasn't going to bargain with God any more, he was just going to surrender to God — and Jacob became Israel, the prince of Israel.

So Jacob was a man who tried to bargain, and still today people try to bargain:

"Lord, if you heal me I'll devote the rest of my life to you."

"Lord, if you'll take this cancer away I'll give more money to missions."

Some preachers encourage this by saying, "You give money to the Lord and he'll bless your business."

That's bargaining with the Lord. But there is nothing you have that God needs, so you are not in a position to bargain.

What you can do is have a covenant with him, but *he* will decide the terms. *He* will make the promises and all you can do is say yes or no.

Now some covenants are what we call *unconditional* which means even if the other party breaks their promises, the covenant will still stand. The party has bound themselves under an obligation, which they cannot break or get out of. But some are *conditional* and they look a little more like a contract because God says, "*If* you do this, I'll do that." However, he still settles the terms. It is still a unilateral bond so it is still a covenant. So whenever you read about a covenant in the Bible, you have to begin by asking, "Is this *unconditional* or *conditional*?"

Please refer to the chart below. Notice, first, that each of the covenants has six things. First of all there is the *party*: Who is the covenant with? Then the *promise* on which the covenant is based — "I will." That is the most frequent thing God says when making a covenant, all the way through the Bible.

The third thing we ask is: Does God expect anything in return? Is there a *proviso* attached to the covenant?

Then: Is there a *penalty* attached which will punish us if we don't keep the covenant?

Then: How long will it last – what *period* does this promise cover?

Finally: What is God's *purpose* in making the covenant?

BIBLICAL COVENANTS	PARTY Who with?	PROMISE (I will...) What offered?	PROVISO What expected?	PENALTY If failed?	PERIOD How long for?	PURPOSE Why?
NOAHIC	Noah & family ON ARARAT	SURVIVAL INTERNATIONAL Seasons Sun & rain	SANCTITY OF LIFE Human Animals	(unconditional)	PERMANENT while earth remains	People available for adoption into God's family
ABRAHAMIC	ABRAHAM + son ISAAC grandson JACOB (patriarchs) IN CANAAN	SELECTION NATIONAL Seed Land (ownership) INTERNATIONAL Blessing for all families on earth	FAITH CIRCUMCISION BLESSED If bless Israel	CUT OFF* CURSED If curse Israel	PERMANENT for ever	A people on earth to mediate God's blessing to others "a kingdom of priests"
MOSAIC (OLD)	MOSES + 12 tribes of ISRAEL ON SINAI	SECURITY NATIONAL Provision Protection Land (occupation)	OBEDIENCE to laws BLESSINGS Health, Prosperity	DISOBEDIENCE of laws CURSES Disasters Occupation, Exile	TEMPORARY until Messiah comes	A demonstration of divine righteousness and need for forgiveness
DAVIDIC	DAVID, king of Israel IN JERUSALEM	SOVEREIGNTY NATIONAL King of Jews INTERNATIONAL King of Gentiles (nations)	MANY SONS if keep covenant SUCCESSION ONE SON "anointed one" HEBREW = Messiah GREEK = Christ	SHORT REIGN (unconditional)	TEMPORARY until Messiah comes PERMANENT for ever	A visible kingdom of God on earth, ruled by his Son
MESSIANIC (NEW)	Announced by (OT) ISAIAH, JEREMIAH, EZEKIEL Achieved by (NT) JESUS' death resurrection, ascension IN JERUSALEM	SALVATION INTERNATIONAL Some Jews Many Gentiles All Israel [FORGIVENESS] [HOLINESS]	REPENTANCE FAITH(FULNESS) BAPTISM Obedience to the gospel	CUT OFF* Eternal loss HELL	PERMANENT for ever Eternal life NEW HEAVEN AND EARTH	Righteous subjects of the kingdom of God, free from sin.

There are *five* covenants we are going to consider. We call each one after the name of the person with whom God made it. So we call the covenant with Noah the *Noahic* covenant. Then God made another with Abraham and we call it the *Abrahamic* covenant. Then he made one with Moses – the *Mosaic* covenant – then the one he made with King David, the *Davidic*, and finally there is the one he made through Christ, the *Messianic*.

These are the five covenants around which the whole Bible story revolves. I want you to notice already that only one of those is called the *old* covenant and that is the *Mosaic*. Only one of them is called the *new* covenant and that is the *Messianic*. That is enlightening to begin with, because the words "covenant" and "testament" are, of course, the same. It is a tragedy that the two parts of our Bible were ever called the *Old* Testament and the *New* Testament, meaning the *old covenant* and the *new covenant,* which gives the wrong impression — that there are only two covenants in the Bible, the old one and the new one, whereas that is not the picture at all. This has misled a lot of people into thinking that the Old Testament is out of date and past its "sell-by" date. There are many Christians today who are not studying the Old Testament. They are studying the New but not the Old because they think it is *old*, out of date.

3

The Covenant with Noah

The whole thing is a very sad business, and the account of it includes the saddest verse in the entire Bible: "God regretted that he had made man." God was sorry that he had made us. I have been in courtrooms where parents have said, "We wish we'd never had children."

When the children have gone wrong and messed up their lives and got into vice and crime, sometimes parents have said to me, "We wish we'd never had them." That is a terrible thing for parents to say, but God said it. It was a particularly decadent point in human history. The earth was filled with violence and that is what happens when people get away from God. Violence spreads so quickly, society becomes less and less safe and old people can't walk the streets in safety. That is one result of getting away from God.

If violence was one of the things that had filled the earth when God regretted making us, the other thing was kinky sex, and of course they go together. Perverted sex and violence are sisters if you like—they each lead to the other because they are both treating people as objects and not as subjects; as things, not as people. The whole of society at that time had become riddled with perverted sex and violence. It even makes this incredible statement in Genesis chapter 6: "Every imagination of man's heart was only evil continually." What a statement! The only thing people could think about was how to do something bad – how to do something cruel, barbaric. The perverted sex was taking a particularly horrible turn. Angels were having sex with human women. You see, God has made the orders of life very clearly. We are here as human beings, animals are below us, and angels are above us. They are superior to us in strength and intelligence. They are a higher form of life. The world seems to find it difficult to believe in angels but the Bible certainly does, all the way through.

So we have animals, humans, angels – all created by God. God has absolutely forbidden sex between those three different orders of life, whether it is between humans and animals – which is now featuring on video nasties – or humans and angels. To God, those are disgusting relationships, as also are sexual relationships between men and men and between women and women. God has ordered life to operate in his way, and what was happening in Noah's day was that angels and human women were having intercourse and it was producing hybrids of a particularly repelling kind. The Hebrew word is *nephilim*, but we really don't know what it means. It is sometimes translated as "giants", or it means grotesque creatures, ugly hybrids.

Now God was looking down on all that—a world of violence and perverted sex, with every imagination of man's heart only evil continually. That is when it says, "God regretted that he had made man." He made a decision to wipe the whole lot out. What a terrible decision, but he found one man who was living right and who had taught his family to live right, and he had a wife, three sons, and three daughters-in-law. Because that man's influence on his family was such, God said, "I'm not going to destroy them." He told the man to build a boat, a crazy thing to do in the middle of the land, and you know the rest of the story—Noah was saved. When Noah came out of the ark, God made the first covenant with man and he promised never to do that again while the earth remained.

The only reason God isn't wiping us out now is that he has kept his promise. People think he doesn't care about all the evil in the world, that he should get rid of it. I am amused when people say to me, "Why doesn't God destroy all the wicked people in the world and then the rest of us could live in peace and happiness and comfort?" There is something a little wrong with that thinking. If God destroyed right now all the evil people in the world who are spoiling it for themselves and other people, and for him, I wouldn't be here to write this, and there would be nobody to sit down to read it either! We are always so sure that it is the *other* people who are messing up the world and really making life intolerable for the rest of us. That's how we think. It is always somebody else, "Lord get rid of *them*." But we ourselves are part of the problem.

So what was God wanting from us? Why did he create the human race? Have you ever asked that question? There is a very simple answer. God already had one son and he enjoyed him so much that he wanted a bigger family. I cannot put it more simply than that—it is why God made you. He wanted you in his family. He wanted a relationship with you, a loving relationship. He wanted you to enjoy what his son already enjoyed in the Father's family. That is why he made us, but what a terrible disappointment to him, the way we turned out. Millions don't even care about him, they can live without him, never think about him, certainly don't even give him thanks. One of the most serious sins in the Bible is not to say thank you. God once destroyed people who grumbled about the food he gave them. They were just not grateful. Do you realise how serious a sin it is to take things from God that he freely gives us and never to bother to say thank you? How would you feel as a parent or as a friend if you gave something to somebody quite regularly and they never said thank you? In Romans chapter 1 it is listed as a serious sin that we do not say thank you to God. Thank you, Lord, for today. Thank you, Lord, for my health. Thank you, Lord.

My wife introduced me to a bad habit when we married. She can't get going in the morning without her early cup of tea. Now if I wake up early and I feel like a Christian, I go down and make the tea, but if I don't feel like a Christian I let her go down and make the tea. I dare not tell you the ratio between the two because I don't often feel like a Christian first thing! Bottles of milk are delivered to our front door every day. So if I go down to make the tea I walk to the front door and pick up these often freezing bottles and remember a verse from the book of Lamentations which says, "Your mercies are fresh every morning." As I carry the fresh milk I say, "Lord, thank you for your mercies." I am in my eighty-third year, with one foot in the grave and the other on a banana skin, but never mind, I've got my health. That is a mercy and I can say, "Thank you, Lord." I've got work to do. I'm working as hard now as I ever did. Thank you, Lord, I have work to do. The only trouble with working for the Lord is that he's a wonderful boss and provides for all your needs but he doesn't have a retirement scheme. (When I said that to a friend of mine, he replied, "Oh yes he does, he has a marvellous one, in fact it's out of this world!") My wife and I have a roof over our heads. What a mercy! "Thank you, Lord."

Every day there are things we need to say thank you for, and we can go whole days without remembering —what an insult to Almighty God. That was part of the situation in the time of Noah's flood. So when Noah and his family, just eight of them, got out of the ark into a world in which the environment had been destroyed, and in which they would have to start again from scratch, God said, "I'll never do it again. I make you a solemn promise that I will always sustain the human race as long as there is an earth that they live on. There will always be springtime and harvest, summer and winter." And of course the two things we need to live are light and moisture, sun and rain. God has promised not only to give us the seasons but to send his sun on the good and the evil, and his rain on the just and unjust.

I love the little poem, *"The rain it raineth on the just and on the unjust fella; but it raineth more so on the just, because the unjust has the just's umbrella."* Work that out for yourself, but God is giving the sun and rain to every human being on earth. Did you know there is enough food in the world every single year for everybody to have their 2,500 calories every day? I was being interviewed on the Australian radio station ABC, and the interviewer said to me, "How can you believe in a good God when children in Ethiopia are starving?" He highlighted all those around the world who go to bed hungry – that is a third of the human race – and another third who go to bed starving. He asked, "How can you believe in a good God?"

I replied, "Actually, I've just seen the United Nations Food Organization figures for last year, and as in every year previously there has been enough food in the world for every single person. Even with the exponential growth in population, God has promised to sustain the human race and keep us alive. It will go up every year. Then why are people hungry and why are people starving? The answer is very simple: *we will not share it*. It is as simple as that. One part of the world is obese and fighting flab and trying to get thinner, and the other part of the world is too thin. Whose fault is that? It's almost as if a father got the deep freeze, locked it up and said, 'God, my children are starving and I blame you.' How foolish to blame God for famine when we will not share what food he has given. But he has promised to keep the seasons going."

The Noahic covenant is still operating. If it wasn't,

we wouldn't be here. We wouldn't have any food to eat. There wouldn't be buds on the trees in springtime unless the Noahic covenant was still in operation. God is still sending his sun on the good and the evil and his rain on the just and unjust.

Look again at the Noahic covenant on the chart. Notice what appears along the top row. Not only was this covenant made with Noah, but through him with the *whole human race*. It was made on Mount Ararat when the ark came to rest after the flood. The promise is basically one of *survival*, that the human race would be kept going by God, that he would keep the food supplied. *It was an international covenant because it was made with everybody.*

It is not a Jewish covenant at all – it is with everybody including the Jews of course, but all the Gentile nations belong to this covenant. The seasons would continue, the sun and rain would continue. What was *expected of us* by God? He didn't make anything a condition. It was an *unconditional* covenant. Therefore, whether we do what God hopes we will do or not, he will go on keeping his side of the covenant. But he did expect certain things of us, and since he promised the survival of life, he expected us to *treat life with respect*. He makes two things quite clear in Genesis chapter 9, one connected with human life and the other connected with animal life. From now on, animals could be used as meat, but they must be properly slaughtered, and the way that was done in those days was that the blood must be drained. You must be absolutely sure that the flesh is dead before you eat it. So the blood was drained so that nobody was tempted to eat live flesh. That would be to lose respect for animal life.

But when we come to human life, God expected us to treat human life as sacred, as something in the image of God. However bad a person may be, they are made in the image of God. They are sacred, therefore to commit murder is sacrilege. If we are going to maintain the sacredness of life, God tells us he expects capital punishment for murder.

Many countries in the world no longer have capital punishment for murder. In America some states do and some don't.

God says, "I will sustain life but you treat it as sacred." The UK abolished capital punishment for murder in the 1960s, and as soon as that happened I said to my wife, "We've lost the sacredness of life." Murder is now simply theft, and the punishment for it is the same as for serious theft. It is no longer regarded as sacrilege. It is simply regarded as stealing a life and therefore life imprisonment is the punishment, and that rarely means the whole of life now. I added, "The next thing will be abortion and after that will come euthanasia – it's bound to follow." Once you no longer see life as sacred, in the image of God, then you will destroy your own youngsters, you will destroy the elderly once they've become useless, and sure enough it's happening right now. We have lost the sacredness of life.

That was not a *condition* of the covenant, otherwise God would not be feeding us now. It was an expectancy that he had hoped would follow: that we would treat animal life and human life with respect – and human life as sacred in the image of God. Unfortunately, we have been so brainwashed by the theory of evolution into thinking we are simply animals that we no longer draw a clear distinction between animals and humans, but in the Bible they are very different. Animals do not bear the image of God. We do, and that is why murder is sacrilege, and a life taken should be paid for with another life taken. But even though we no longer keep this very widely, God keeps his covenant. It was unconditional, and we know exactly how long it will last—*as long as the earth remains*. The earth is still here and we are still here. God has kept his promise. Now why did he promise to do that? Because if he hadn't he would never get his family. He wants sons and daughters in his family. He wants human beings to relate to him. He constantly says in the Bible, all the way through, "I will be their God and they will be my people." That's what he wanted: a bigger family, relationships.

So he has to preserve the human race or he won't get any more in his family — that's the basic purpose. That's why you're here, that's why I'm here. I'm not here to enjoy myself and pursue happiness. That might be in the American constitution but it is not why God put you here. He put you here to find him and be his family, and until you discover that, you will not find the real purpose of life because there isn't another.

Furthermore, he has given himself a reminder to keep his word. You have seen it — a rainbow. Whenever sun and rain come together, we see that beautiful rainbow. It is God's wedding ring, his covenant ring. He doesn't say, "When *you* see that rainbow remember that promise." He says, "When *I* see the rainbow I'll remember my promise. That's a reminder to me to keep the human race alive." This he has promised to do. He did destroy it once and we need to remember that he did, and that he could do it again. But he has kept his promise to keep us going. The reason why he has done that is very simple: because he wants a family. He is determined to have a family, but if he is going to get one he will have to make some rather different covenants because the Noahic covenant will not of itself give God a family. It will give him a *potential* family, but not an *actual* one.

4

The Covenant with Abraham

We turn to the next covenant God made, rather later than the Noahic covenant. He made it with a dear old man who was living in a brick built house with lovely fireplaces and bedrooms upstairs – I kid you not! If you go to Ur of the Chaldees you can see the most sophisticated brick houses. I got a photograph of one and showed it to my wife and said, "How would you like to live in that house?" She said, "It's a bit old fashioned." I said, "It should be, it's four thousand years old."

So we are shown an old man who lived in a comfortable brick house with lovely fireplaces, and God said, "I want you to live in a tent for the rest of your life." I don't know many eighty-year-old men who would leave a nice house and live in a tent for the rest of their lives, and not only live in a tent but go far away to a country they had never seen, leave their friends behind, and just go. That old man went. "Abraham is the father of us all," says the Bible, and he was – just an old man leaving a pagan place with its weird gods and goddesses, and setting off on a long trek at that age, and with his elderly wife too. Abraham trusted and obeyed God and set out on the journey, and God said, "I'm going to make a covenant with you." It was an amazing covenant – not this time of *survival* but of *selection*, to choose Abraham and his descendants to be special people.

God repeated the covenant with his son Isaac and his grandson Jacob. With three generations of men, God married them with a 'testament' – and a covenant in a sense is, as we have seen, a marriage. It is an "I will." Now why did God choose them? Were they better than everyone else? No. In fact, they weren't perfect at all. Each of the three men lied, deceiving others to save their own skin. You read the story. The only thing about them that made them unique was that *they did what God told them*. They trusted and obeyed God's Word – that's all. For that reason God made a relationship with them, and amazingly God took their three names into his name and from then on was known as God of Abraham, Isaac, and Jacob.

He is still the God of those three men who obeyed him and became his heirs. He said, "I'm leaving you a land in the middle of the world that's yours forever."

The interesting thing is, though Abraham never owned it, he left it in his will to his son. Isaac never owned it, and he left it in his will to his son. They passed down the title deeds of that land from generation to generation. What faith to leave somebody something you haven't got yet, but which you have been promised! That's faith, isn't it? I have only made a will for what I have but I haven't left anything in my will that I haven't got. Abraham did, Isaac did, Jacob did—those three men are tied forever into God.

Jesus said, "They're still alive. They're not dead." I've seen their tombs in Hebron but they're not in the tombs. Abraham and Isaac and Jacob are alive now if you believe what Jesus said, and they will be alive at the end of history. One day, the Bible says, we shall sit down with Abraham and Isaac and Jacob in the kingdom and have a banquet. I can't resist adding that Jesus will be the waiter serving the meal (Luke 12:37). What an amazing sight: sitting down – "Abraham, hello," and Isaac, yes, and Jacob – and Jesus says, "Here's your meal." I just can't cope with that. I feel a bit like Peter. "You'll never wash my feet" – "No, come on, let me serve the meal, Jesus." "No ," Jesus will say, "I'm serving, it's your banquet."

Well now, God was selecting these three men and their descendants. This covenant was in Canaan, the land that was promised to them, and it had a national and an international aspect. The national aspect was that God would give Abraham seed even though he was so old and his wife was way past childbearing. God said, "I'll see that you get seed and I will give you a land in which they can live forever." That was the promise, that was the covenant—that's the national side of it.

The little word "ownership" is significant because the ownership is not conditional, it is unconditional. It will forever belong to the Jewish people.

But there was also an international side to it, which was that "Through you all the families of the earth will be blessed."

This is what philosophers call the scandal of particularity. This was God's way of working: to choose one people, and through them bless all the others.

We had three children and I used to bring them confectionery every Saturday – it was just a little family custom. I could do it one of two ways: either give all the sweets to one of them and say "Share those with the other two," or give them each a bag of their own.

In the second case we had peace in the house; in the first case we had arguments, "You got one more than me, it's not fair." But that's the way God chose. He didn't choose to bless the Americans and the Chinese and the Indians and the British. He said, "I'm giving it to you Jews, now you share it with everybody else." That is why we are all dependent on the Jewish people. We owe them so much. We wouldn't have a Bible but for the Jewish people. There wouldn't be a church but for the Jewish people. Everything that I value most I owe to the Jewish people—that's how God works. I am sure you know the little poem: *How odd of God to choose the Jews...*, and then another poet added another verse because he thought it was too short, *But odder still for those who choose the Jewish God and scorn the Jews.* Yet many Christians do that. At best they ignore the Jewish people; at worst, well I had better not say more. Jews have suffered more in Christian countries than in Muslim countries. The Holocaust happened in a country that was half Protestant and half Catholic. It is to the shame of the church that the church has caused the Jews to suffer so deeply and so greatly—shame on us.

So there is the international side of the Abrahamic covenant: "Through you all the families of the earth will be blessed."

But there was another codicil to God's will here. He said this, "Everyone who blesses your descendants I will bless, but everyone who curses your descendants I will curse." For God is a God who curses as well as blesses. He is a God who hates as well as loves. He is a God who kills as well as heals. He is a God of goodness *and* severity and we need to remember that.

Our attitude to the people he chose will determine his attitude to us. Bless a Jew and the God of Israel will bless you. Curse them and you'll be cursed.

I have seen that happen in my lifetime to a nation and to individuals. The God who made the whole universe is the God of Israel – the God of Abraham, Isaac, and Jacob. He has tied himself to them and we need to remember that constantly.

Now was there a proviso – a condition? The answer is yes, there was. The condition for his descendants was that they be circumcised – that simple operation of the removal of the foreskin, significantly from the organ of reproduction. They would bear in their body that special mark down through the generations. Abraham was told: If any of your descendants refuses to be circumcised, or is not circumcised for any reason, they are out of the covenant. It was a firm condition and it was the only condition that was made (Genesis 17:14).

Now I put it this way: every Jew who is circumcised is carrying the title deeds to the Promised Land inside his trousers — that's the truth. If he bears that mark then he is a descendant of Abraham who belongs to the land and the land belongs to him. That's at the root of the problems in the Middle East right now, but we must listen to what God says, and not just what people are saying, about the Middle East.

How long does this covenant last? It is for ever. The purpose of God in making this covenant was that he now had a channel through whom he could communicate to the whole world. He placed them in the middle of the world in the Promised Land to demonstrate how blessed people are if they live God's way and how cursed they are if they don't. The Jews have been a demonstration of both down through the centuries. No nation has been more blessed than the Jewish and no nation has been more cursed than the Jewish. They are a living demonstration of God. When King Louis of France asked Pascal to give him one proof of the existence of God, the latter replied, "Your majesty, the Jews." That, I think, is a wonderful answer. Study the history of the Jews and try to explain any of it without God and you have a job on your hands. They are a demonstration to the world.

5

The Covenant with Moses (old)

The Mosaic covenant was made at Mount Sinai 430 years after Abraham, and this covenant concerned the *occupation* of the land whereas the Abrahamic gave them the *ownership* of the land for ever. That doesn't mean that there weren't conditions of occupying it, and God gave laws covering their family life, their marriages, their deaths, their clothes, their food, their sewage disposal, bye-laws galore. There were 613 of them – ten big ones we know as the Ten Command-ments, but 603 others covering every aspect of their life. This was how they were to live a holy, healthy, happy life.

"If you live this way I will bless the land, it will be fertile. I will bless your bodies, there will be no disease among you. There will be no poverty among you." Wonderful covenant, but the downside is, "If you don't live my way then I will curse you; I will send pestilence, drought, disease on your crops, locusts to eat them up; I'll send earthquakes; I'll send invaders to raid your country. If that still doesn't work, if you still go on the wrong way, I'll let them come in and occupy the country, and finally, if you still refuse to live my way you leave the country and I send you into exile."

All that happened. Read your Old Testament. It is the story of a people who stubbornly refused to live God's way. They were stiff-necked, stubborn. It's a tragic story. It took them a thousand years to get all the Promised Land and only five hundred to lose it all.

Now this was the *Mosaic* covenant, which was purely national and was a covenant of *security* in the land, with those provisos.

Now God keeps his promises – whether to bless or to curse – right up to today. If you read Deuteronomy 28, the list of curses that God would bring when they didn't live his way, you are reading the story of the Holocaust just seventy years ago. It is an incredible account of what happened in Nazi Germany written down three thousand and more years ago. God kept his promise to them. That is quite a severe thing to say because the one thing the Jews debate is, "Where was God in the Holocaust?" I've only heard one Jew who ever dared to say God was cursing his people and that was Art Katz.

But you don't play games with God. He is serious. He means what he says and he has promised blessing and curse, not just to the Jews but to the whole human race. One day, the Lord Jesus will divide the nations like a shepherd divides the sheep and the goats, and he will say to those on one hand, "Come you blessed of my Father, inherit the kingdom." To the others he will say, "Depart from me, you cursed." Jesus himself will bless and curse the whole world.

The Mosaic covenant was temporary. It was really only intended until the Messiah came, so all those laws of Moses were temporary — and that is a very important point to make (see Galatians 3:23–25). It was so that they would be this demonstration of how blessed and how cursed a nation could be if it either lived God's way or lived its own way. The 'national' anthem of living our own way is, "*I did it my way.*" That is the essence of sin, and that is what God cannot cope with. He gave us life, he told us how to live it — how to be healthy and happy, how to be his heirs, and most of us don't even want to know!

Unless you are careful you find yourself being put back under that Jewish covenant, and even preachers make that mistake. To mention just one example — if you've been told you must tithe your income you have been put back under the one covenant that doesn't affect you. In the new covenant you *give*, not *tithe*. There is no tax in the new covenant. In fact it says, "God loves a cheerful giver" – which does not mean when the collection plate comes around, put a grin on! It does mean that God is not interested in your money unless you want to give it. For many people a tithe would be far too small for how generous they feel toward the Lord in gratitude, and for others it might be far too big. For a single mother caring for children having been deserted by a husband, the tithe would be too much. God doesn't want your money unless you want to give it. That's what "The Lord loves a cheerful giver" means. He loves a sacrificial giver and a regular giver, and a cheerful giver above all. That's just an aside but it is an illustration of how we can get back into the wrong covenant because that tithing covenant was part of the one that applies to the Jewish people and, thank God, not to me.

To illustrate that, there was a time some years ago where Israeli and Arab believers in Israel got together and found that they didn't have enough in common to really get together and they were soon arguing with each other. They felt the need to have someone from right outside come and bang their heads together and say, "Get it together." They unanimously suggested me, phoned me and said, "Will you please come straight out to Israel? We need you."

It is pretty expensive if you buy a ticket at the last minute. I found out it would be about £680. So I said,

"I haven't got that money and I can't ask you for that." What happened was that the young Israel and Arab believers got together, turned their pockets out, put their money together, and collected shekels to the equivalent of £120. Meanwhile, I went to Luton Airport and asked the person at the ticket counter, "Have you any charter flights going to Israel?"

"Yes, there's one just about to leave," they replied.

"Could you put me on that?"

The reply came, "No, every seat is full."

I said, "Are you sure you can't put me on that?"

"Well, you can have one of the crew's seats – you know, those tip-up seats that face backwards that the cabin crew sit on. Would you mind one of those? They're not very comfortable."

"How much will you charge me?"

"£120."

It was the exact amount that the young people in Israel had collected, so I got on the plane and sat backwards, facing a row of people. I noticed that I was the only Gentile on the plane. All the other passengers looked as though they were popping over to Jerusalem to visit their folk. I noticed the three sitting in front of me were rabbis, so we had a good kosher meal and then I thought, "Well, let's have a conversation." So I said to the first rabbi, "Do you keep the law of Moses?"

"Of course I do."

I said, "Well what about this one?"

"Well, no, we don't keep that one. We keep something else instead."

"Oh, you don't keep all the laws of Moses?"

Then I said to the second, "Do you keep the law of Moses?"

"Oh yes, we all keep the law."

I said, "Well, what about this one?"

"You see, we can't keep that one because we don't have a temple."

"Oh, you don't keep all the laws of Moses."

With the third rabbi there was the same response.

Finally, the first one looked me in the eye and said, "What are you – Orthodox? Liberal? Reformed Jew?"

I said, "No, none of those."

Then he said, "I know who you are. You're a Christian. You don't think you need to keep the law of Moses."

I said, "No, that's right. And what a relief to me, none of the three of you is keeping the laws of Moses!"

Unfortunately, soon afterwards we landed at what is now Ben Gurion Airport and the conversation finished.

It is the law of Moses that is for Jews. When you put yourself under the law of Moses you are in problems if you are a Gentile. We will return to that later, but that is what happens when you mix up the covenants of scripture. Each covenant is for a particular people, a particular purpose, for a particular period, and we need to ask all these questions about the different covenants.

6

The Covenant with David

The covenant God made with King David was about *succession*. The kingdom of Israel under David reached its peak, its greatest borders. Most if not all of the Promised Land was theirs. They had peace. The Philistines were defeated. Other nations had been drawn into the kingdom of David, which was now an empire, and still today Jews look back to the time of David as the best of their history. I wear two rings and they both have the name David in Hebrew inscribed on them. One was given to me by my wife on our twenty-fifth wedding anniversary, and I watched a little Jew in Jerusalem make it. He engraved the walls of Jerusalem on it, and my name on the top. My wife gave me this to remind me to be a 'watchman on the wall'.

The other ring was discovered in London when the foundations were being dug for a new block of apartments. It was found that they were digging in an old Jewish cemetery. Along with the bones they found a ring with the name David on it and gave it to me. I am very grateful for that. I don't know who it belonged to, simply that it belonged to a Jew called David long ago.

When Israel was at the peak of its powers, God made a covenant with David and, in the last words of David on his deathbed, he thanked God for that covenant. It was a mixture of the national and the international. On the national side, God promised successors who would sit on his throne if they kept the commandments of God.

But there was another part to the promise: that one day there would be a son of David who would sit on David's throne forever, and would not only be king of the Jews but king of the whole world, of all the nations—that's the Davidic covenant. What a covenant! We know who that son was. It was the Messiah through whom the new covenant would be established, the anointed one. The *anointed one* in Hebrew is *Maschiah*, from which we get *Messiah*. In Greek it is *Christos*, from which we get *Christ*. That isn't Jesus' surname, it means Messiah. I wish we would use it instead of "Christ". It would remind us that he is Jewish, and that he is fulfilling the Jewish covenants. If, instead of saying "the Lord Jesus Christ", we say, "the Lord Jesus, Messiah" then we are really pointing to the meaning: king of the Jews.

The short reign of many sons was conditional on their keeping the commandments, but the one reign of the one Son was unconditional and would last forever. The others would be temporary kings on David's throne, but once Jesus came he was the permanent King. This was to make visible the kingdom of God on earth. We were not made for democracy — that is alien to human nature. I remember seeing the film *The Ten Commandments* by Cecil B. DeMille. He appeared on the screen in the beginning and said, "This film is about the beginnings of democracy." I thought, "Democracy? Don't you know your Bible? There's not a trace of democracy in the Bible." Winston Churchill said, "Democracy is the worst possible form of government except all the others," which was quite a profound statement if you think it through. We were not made for democratic elections, political parties and government. We were made to live in a kingdom under a king who would make the rules. Many people think that is a horrible idea, but I could persuade them in two minutes to change their minds. You see, the problem with kings is that most of them are bad, power goes to their heads, they are corrupted and bribed, and it all goes wrong.

But what if I could find you a king who had laid down his life for everybody, and who had a concern for the poor especially – someone who was not interested in power, wealth or fame but wanted to serve everybody, even at the cost of his own life. Now would you like such a king? The answer is that we've found one! In Acts the early Christians were persecuted because they said, "There is another king." That is our gospel: we have found the perfect king – and one day he will be the king over every nation.

Tell others that one day they will have a king – and he will be Jewish. That is the truth, because the Davidic covenant will be fulfilled, and has been. We have found the perfect person to rule over us, whose service is perfect freedom.

In the next chapter we will think about the new covenant and how it affects all the others we have considered.

7

The Messianic Covenant (new)

The following passage combines all I have been teaching here – linking Israel and the 'new' covenant.

"The time is coming," declares the LORD, "when I will make a new covenant with the house of Israel and with the house of Judah. It will not be like the covenant I made with their forefathers when I took them by the hand to lead them out of Egypt, because they broke my covenant, though I was a husband to them," declares the LORD. "This is the covenant I will make with the house of Israel after that time," declares the LORD. "I will put my law in their minds and write it on their hearts. I will be their God, and they will be my people. No longer will a man teach his neighbour, or a man his brother, saying, 'Know the LORD,' because they will all know me, from the least of them to the greatest," declares the LORD. "For I will forgive their wickedness and will remember their sins no more." This is what the LORD says, he who appoints the sun to shine by day, who decrees the moon and stars to shine by night, who stirs up the sea so that its waves roar – the LORD Almighty is his name: "Only if these decrees vanish from my sight," declares the LORD, "will the descendants of Israel ever cease to be a nation before me." This is what the LORD says: "Only if the heavens above can be measured and the foundations of the earth below be searched out will I reject all the descendants of Israel because of all they have done," declares the LORD.

Jeremiah 31:31–37 NIV

We are thinking about five covenants in the Bible and we have looked at four of them. We have noted that all five covenants can be found in what we call the Old Testament and all five covenants can be found in the New. I emphasise that, because our Bibles have been divided into the Old and New Testaments, and that is very misleading—I don't know who put those titles in but it was a mistake. I am quite sure God did not inspire the names because "testament" and "covenant" are the same word.

When part of your Bible is called the *old* covenant or *Old* Testament and half is called the *New*, that gives you the impression that there are only two, and that

everything under the old is obsolete and past its "sell
by date", and everything in the "New" is different and
special and fresh, and we should concentrate on the
New. Nothing could be a greater mistake. I hope you
read the whole Bible right through (from "generation"
to "revolution"!) – from beginning to end.

I remember going into a little cottage and finding an
old man sitting by the fire, and he was reading his Bible.
Every time I went to see him he was reading his Bible,
and I said to him, "How often have you read the Bible?

He replied, "Many times."

"How many times?"

"Eighteen times."

"Why do you read it right through?" I continued. Still
a young man myself, I had never done that.

He answered, "Because I don't want to miss
anything." I like that, don't you?

Then there was an old lady reading her Bible whom
I asked, "Why are you reading your Bible?"

She said, "I'm swotting for my finals," which is quite
a neat answer.

We have mentioned that all five covenants are in
the Old Testament, all five are in the New, but of these
five only one is called the old covenant and only one
is called the new covenant, and the latter has replaced
the former. The new one we call the *Messianic* because

it was established by Jesus himself – the Messiah, the Christ. Now let us look at the new covenant. It is an exciting one.

THE "NEW" COVENANT – completed

1. Announced in the Old Testament

JEREMIAH – WHAT?   **FATHER**
a. Inclination
           Therefore: internal
b. Intimacy   individual
c. Innocence   I

ISAIAH – WHO?   **SON**
a. Supreme sovereign
b. Suffering servant   I

EZEKIEL – HOW?   **HOLY SPIRIT**
a. Human spirit renewed
b. Holy Spirit received

2. Achieved in the New Testament

LORD JESUS CHRIST
a. Atonement – to take away our sins
                   – resurrection between
b. Ascension – to fill us with the Spirit

THE HOLY SPIRIT
a. Baptised in – once
b. Filled with – continually

NEW COVENANT PEOPLE
a. Body of Christ – his flock and family
b. Fellowship of the Spirit – his gifts and fruit

It was *announced* in the Old Testament so it had been announced for a long time before it was established, and it was announced by three of the prophets in the Old Testament: Jeremiah, Isaiah, and Ezekiel. They each contributed a different angle on this new covenant that God would make, which would be so very different from and so much better than the old covenant, which was made with Moses on Mount Sinai. In fact, Jeremiah chapter 31 said, "It will *not* be like the covenant I made with you when I brought you out of Egypt" —that would be the one on Sinai; this one would be very different.

Jeremiah announced *what* it would be, what would be its conditions/provisions. Then Isaiah announced *who* would bring it and establish it. Ezekiel announced *how* it would work. When you put those three together you get a wonderful picture of what this new covenant was going to be like.

Let us begin, then, with Jeremiah. What is the new covenant? The first thing to note is *inclination*. What do I mean by that? This new covenant would be written not on tablets of stone but *in people's minds and in their hearts*. It would be written *inside* people and not *outside* people. What does that mean?

It means that they would not just be told how to live but would be given a desire to live that way; they would *want* to live right, and that is the difference. The old covenant told them how to live but didn't give them an incentive. When you face people with "Thou shalt not..." there is something inside human nature that wants to go and do it—that's the problem with the old covenant, although its commandments were good, as were the Ten Commandments.

A little boy went to school the first day and his teacher said, "What's your name?" He said, "Johnny Don't." She said, "I'm sure that's not your name." He said, "But that's what mummy always calls me: "Johnny, Don't." There was another little boy and he got up from the table before the meal was over and his mother said, "Sit down," and he didn't sit down. So she shouted again, "I said sit down." He still stood up. Then she really got angry and said, "Sit down, or else." He sat down and said, "The outside of me is sitting down but the inside of me is still standing up."

That is about children, but grown-ups are just as bad. I remember a student at Cambridge who hung a notice on the door of his study which read: "Silence, I'm studying." So we all walked past stamping our feet and making a racket in the corridor. Tell somebody not to do a thing and you are inviting them to go and do it. That's human nature because these rules are written outside us, not inside. When the rule is written in your heart and in your mind you want to do it.

In some churches in England they recite the Ten Commandments at a Sunday morning service. The response people are suppose to make after each commandment is: "Lord, incline our hearts to keep this law." The old covenant was dealing with hearts that were inclined not to obey but the new covenant will change the heart and incline it to obey, so you actually find yourself wanting to do good, wanting to be right, wanting to obey God, wanting to do what he says, and wanting to live the way he wants you to live—that's the new covenant. Moses' covenant never did that.

The second thing to note about the new covenant is *intimacy*. Jeremiah teaches that in the new covenant people would all know the Lord personally, not secondhand. They wouldn't have Moses coming down the mountain telling them *about* God, they would *know him*. When you know someone, you know when they are upset *because* you know them. I have lived with my wife now for over fifty years. I know her. She doesn't have to tell me when I'm in the doghouse, I know; she just goes quiet.

Normally when I go overseas I phone her and say, "I've arrived safely." I went to Australia once, called her and said, "Hello darling, hello?" I said, "Is that you darling?" There was a long pause.

"Yes." Another long pause.

"Are you alright?"

"Yes." Another pause.

"You sure everything's alright?"

"Yes." Yet another.

I thought, "Help. What did I do wrong? I'm sure I kissed her goodbye. What did she ask me to do before I left that I didn't do?" I was really sweating in Australia, then I suddenly realised it was the kind of pause when the satellite message went up and down again. Oh, was I relieved!

You see, she just has to go quiet and I *know*. When you are first married she has to write little notes to you. You come in late and there's a little note on the kitchen table: *Your slippers are in the fridge and your supper's in the dog and I've gone to bed with a headache*. You know you are in trouble, but she doesn't need to write to me now, because I know her and I can tell as quickly as that, I have upset her, I have grieved her, I did something she didn't want me to do, or I haven't done something she did want me to do—I *know*.

That is how it is in the new covenant between you and the Lord. You know when you have upset him. You know when you have done something he didn't want you to do, you just know because now you know him.

You don't need anybody else to tell you when you

have done something wrong. You *know* and that's a lovely, intimate relationship to have with the Lord.

Innocence is the third characteristic of this new covenant that Jeremiah is talking about, because if there is one thing that spoils a relationship, it is guilt. If you are feeling guilty about something you cannot be relaxed with someone you love. It comes between you. You have got something you don't want them to know. You are hiding a secret from them.

If some husbands took flowers to their wives, they might say, "What have you been up to now?" But to be really forgiven is a lovely experience because you are clean. You are innocent again, and when you are innocent you can give yourself as a little child does – without reservation. So, in this new covenant, Jeremiah says, "God will forgive your sins and remember them no more." God controls his memory, though I cannot control mine. When I have done something wrong I can't forgive myself because I can't forget it. But God can control his "forgetory" – his memory – and he says, "I will remember no more."

Late one Sunday night I was closing the church building and putting the lights out, and I noticed a little old lady sitting in the front row, sobbing her heart out. I sat down next to her and said, "Tell me dear. What's the matter? Why are you so unhappy?"

She said, "Twenty years ago I did the most terrible thing. I'm so ashamed. If my family knew, they wouldn't own me. They'd never speak to me again. If my friends knew, I'd lose all my friends." But she said, "The worst thing is that for all those years I've been asking the Lord to forgive me, and he never has."

I replied, "Oh, you poor soul, for all those years you've been talking about it to the Lord and he doesn't know what you're talking about because the first time you asked his forgiveness he forgave you, and he forgot all about it."

She said, "I can't believe that."

Because, you see, *she* couldn't forget about it so she thought the Lord couldn't either. I had to take her through the Bible, verse by verse, where God says, "I will not remember it." At last she realised the truth and she got up – this old lady who I think must have been in her late seventies – and she danced all the way around the empty church. I just sat and watched her. She was dancing for joy that God had forgotten.

Only God can do that, nobody else can forget—that's why we find it so difficult to forgive each other and certainly it is hard to feel forgiven yourself when you feel you have let yourself down, because you cannot forget. You can bury it in your subconscious but it is amazing how it has a habit of popping up at the most unexpected times. Just a sound or a smell or something reminds you of it, and back it comes again, years later – *but to know that God has forgotten it is something else*.

Sometimes I think that when I see the Lord face to face I will say, "Oh Lord, I really regret some of the things I've done. I'm so sorry I did that." He'll say to me, "Did what, David? I don't recall that." What a miracle—that is forgiveness.

So the new covenant will give you a heart that wants to keep God's laws. The new covenant will give you a knowledge of God so you know straightaway when you have upset him, and the new covenant will give you a clean conscience so that there's nothing between you and him. What a covenant. That's better than the laws of Moses – far, far better.

This new covenant Jeremiah told us about is an *individual* covenant. It is not made with nations but with persons. Your parents may be in the covenant but it doesn't mean you will be, because it is an individual covenant. In fact, a husband may be in it and a wife may not be, or a wife may be in it and a husband may not be. You cannot hide behind anybody else.

In this covenant, you come into it by yourself and God makes a covenant with you as an individual—that's written into Jeremiah 31. And it's an *internal* covenant as well, inside you, written in your heart.

Now let us turn to the prophet Isaiah, who also talked about the new covenant – but he talked about the person who would make it, who would establish it between God and people.

He said two things about this person: in the first half of Isaiah he talked about a supreme sovereign, a king, a ruler. The government would be on his shoulder. He would be the prince of peace; he would be the everlasting Father; he would be a wonderful counsellor; but above all, he would be the conquering king, and that is a very strong picture. But then in the second half of the book the prophet changes his tune and talks about a suffering servant.

You probably know the five songs about the suffering servant but there is one in particular, a most beautiful one, in Isaiah chapter 53. "He was wounded for our transgressions, bruised for our iniquities, the chastisement of our peace was upon him, and by his stripes we are healed." It is a picture of someone suffering terribly, suffering for the sins of his people and not even raising his voice but, like a sheep to the slaughter, remaining dumb while people put him to death. Well we know who that's about, even though it was written a thousand years before Jesus—that is our Saviour.

This is an extraordinary combination: supreme sovereign and suffering servant. The Jews, to this day, cannot get those two things together. They even believe there are probably two Messiahs coming: a Messiah ben Joseph and a Messiah ben David – or Messiah son of Joseph and a Messiah son of David. They are quite mistaken in that. They just cannot get the two things together, but we can because we know that this person is coming twice to the earth: that he has been a suffering servant and that he is coming back again as supreme sovereign. So to us it is the same person but on two visits to planet earth – it is not two different people.

We have noted that one example of a testament or covenant is when you make the last will and testament and leave your property or money to someone else. It is your will. You can change it while you are still alive, but you can't after you die. In fact, that "will" cannot come into effect *until* you die. Up to then it is just a piece of paper, and then what you have willed to your heirs can be given to them.

The New Testament says this about the new covenant – that it could not come into effect for us until the one who established it died. The night before Jesus died, he said, "This is my blood of the new covenant." He had to die so that you could inherit the covenant. That was exactly what happened. By his suffering death, our

Lord Jesus gave us a new covenant. That is why you have communion regularly in church – taking bread and wine to remember. He had to die so that you could have the new covenant. When you drink from the cup you are told, "This is my blood of the new covenant," says Jesus, "Drink it in remembrance of me."

Now we turn to Ezekiel and see what he says about this new covenant. He doesn't say much about *what* it is and nor does he say much about *who* establishes it, but he says a lot about *how* it is going to happen. How can the law be written in our hearts? How can this whole change in us take place? He tells us two vital truths.

First, he says that in the new covenant the human spirit will be made soft and tender; the heart of stone will become a heart of flesh. You will be a softer person a more sensitive person. Your human spirit will change because, basically, when we are sinning we become tough and hard. We don't respond to other people very warmly, but God is going to change all that and the human spirit will be softer inside and then he can write his laws on that softer heart.

The other thing he is going to do is to give his Holy Spirit to people. One thing quite clear is that we will never enjoy the new covenant until we receive the Holy Spirit. That is absolutely essential, so Ezekiel knew – though he was writing hundreds of years before the new covenant was made possible – how it would work by changing the human spirit and giving the Holy Spirit.

All that was said centuries before it happened and in a sense as your read those three prophets you get a glimpse of the Father in Jeremiah, the Son in Isaiah, and the Holy Spirit in Ezekiel.

So even in the Old Testament you are getting a glimpse of the three persons of the godhead who all work together for our good – and you really cannot get anywhere without the Father and the Son and the Holy Spirit. They work together to bring us into the new covenant.

What was *announced* in the Old Testament is *achieved* in the New Testament. It actually happens, and again it is the Lord Jesus Christ who achieves it, first by dying to take away our sins and then ascending to heaven to pour out his Holy Spirit on us, with the resurrection in between.

Without the death, burial, resurrection, and ascension, you and I could never enter the new covenant, but because he did all that on our behalf, we can do so.

But not only the Lord Jesus — we need more than the Lord Jesus to get into the covenant. We need the third person of the Trinity, the Holy Spirit. We need first to be baptised in the Holy Spirit. In every one of the four Gospels we are told right at the beginning. John the Baptist said: I can baptise you in water, but he will baptise you in the Holy Spirit.

Everybody needs two baptisms: a baptism in water and a baptism in the Holy Spirit. I would have to say what John said – I can baptise someone in water; the one thing I cannot do for you is baptise you in the Holy Spirit. The only person who can do that is Jesus Christ.

Have you been baptised in the Holy Spirit? Do you know what that means? One thing it means is to be filled to overflowing with God's Holy Spirit. So how do you know when you are filled to overflowing? How do you know when the fuel tank in your car is full? It overflows! There is a hole at the top of the tank and when the tank is full, it will overflow. I am sure in your bath you will see there is a hole just underneath the taps. To confess a weakness now: I love a hot bath and I can even write a whole book in my head in a hot bath because I am relaxed. I am facing the right way and I've got a dish aerial around me to pick up messages from outer space and I can stay in that bath until it's cold and I'm still thinking thoughts of God. But the trouble is, if I take all the hot water and then jump in, the water goes out of a hole underneath the taps, the "overflow", and it makes a horrible gurgling sound and a little lady downstairs shouts up, "You've taken all the hot water again." That's an overflow. Now did you know that God has given every one of us an overflow? It's a little hole about an inch below your nose, and if you put your finger on the tip of your nose and just work down you'll find your "overflow"!

Whatever you are full of will come out of your mouth. If you are full of fun you will laugh. You can't help it. It overflows.

When you're full of fear, you scream — it comes out.

When you are full of anger you shout.

When you are filled with the Holy Spirit, something is going to come out of your mouth. It might be a totally new language. It could be anything, but you are full to overflowing. I was sitting with a missionary in Brazil in a public park. We were having some sandwiches, a picnic. He said to me, "David I've tried to serve the Lord faithfully. I've been a missionary here for ten years. I have never really seen any miracles. I'm not getting very far and I'm trying to do my best for the Lord" – and I believe he really had. "But I don't think I've ever really been filled with the Holy Spirit. Would you pray for me?"

Well, I just sat there and put a hand on his head and said, "Lord, fill this man to overflowing."

He opened his mouth and yelled, "Hallelujah." Everybody in the park turned around and I sort of carefully turned away from him, and then I said to him,

"Have you ever done that before?"

He replied, "Never; I'm a reserved English man, I would never shout out in public like that." Then he said, "Is that it?"

I said, "I just heard you overflow. That's it."

Within twenty-four hours he had healed two sick people, which he had never done before.

That's what I understand baptism in the Spirit to be – to be filled to overflowing with the Holy Spirit – and that is how you know when you are full up, because you can't keep it in.

I am going to tell you my testimony about how I got filled with the Holy Spirit. There was a man in our church who was the self-appointed "leader of the opposition". Does your church have someone like that? I think God puts one in every church just to keep us on the ball. I got fed up with that man. At everything I suggested, he either said, "We've never done it before and we're not going to try it now" or, "We've done it before and it didn't work." So everything I suggested he flattened. I used to come home from a church meeting and say to my wife, "Oh, Jimmy!" She would say, "Look, all the other members are with you. It's only James." (Jimmy, for short).

Once a year I got wonderful relief from James because he had a weak chest and developed hay fever in the spring, and the doctor would put him to bed for up to six weeks. He could hardly breathe, but I had six weeks where I could do so much in the church without the leader of the opposition. It happened every year. Then this happened again one year, and I thought I must go and see him.

So I went to visit him and all the way there I heard the word James 5, James 5, James 5, and I thought, "Well that's his name, but what's the five?" You may know! In the letter of James, chapter 5 it says, "Is anyone sick? Let him call for the elders, let them anoint him with oil and he will be healed." I thought: I don't want to do it to James. In fact, I had never done it up till then.

When I arrived, I said, "Hello James, how are you?"

He asked, "What do you think about James 5?"

I replied, "Why do you ask?"

"I want you to do it to me. I've got to go to Switzerland on business on Thursday morning and the doctors have put me in bed for at least three weeks."

There he was, lying flat on the bed with a grey face, gasping for breath, with his lungs full up.

"Will you come and do that?"

I said, "I'll pray about it."

That's a wonderful get out, isn't it? I went home and tried to pray about it. "Lord, please tell me why I shouldn't do this. There must be a good reason." But the heavens were like brass and I got no answer.

On the Wednesday his wife phoned me and said, "James says are you coming to anoint him with oil?"

I agreed, "All right, I'll come tonight and I'll bring some of the other leaders." I went out and bought a big bottle of olive oil. Then, that night, I set off. In his bedroom there he was: lying there, gasping for breath. So I opened the Bible at James 5 and we went through it like a car manual, just doing each thing it said. Well, the first thing it said was: confess your sins to one another. So I thought we had better start at the beginning and said, "James, I've never liked you." He said, "That's mutual." So we dealt with that.

Then it says to pray, so we prayed. Then it said anoint with oil so I got the olive oil bottle, took the top off and poured it all over his head. Guess what happened —absolutely nothing! He lay there gasping, and I wondered, "Why did I get into this?" I turned to run out of the bedroom but thought, "He'll be worse than ever now. He'll think nothing of me now." Reaching the door, I asked, "Have you still got your ticket for Switzerland for tomorrow?"

"Of course."

"I'll run you to the airport," I offered.

Then I ran, and didn't sleep all night.

The next morning I didn't want to know him. I wished

I had never been, and so I tried to prepare a sermon, trying to forget him.

The telephone rang. When I picked it up, a voice said, "Hello, James here. Can you pick me up and take me to the airport?"

"Are you alright James?" I asked.

"Yes, I'm fine."

"What happened?"

He said, "In the middle of the night it was as if two hands squeezed my chest. I coughed up a bucket full of liquid from my lungs and I could breathe."

"Have you been to the doctor?" I asked.

"Yes, and the doctor says I'm fine. In fact, I have even been to have a haircut. The barber said, 'I'm afraid I'll have to wash your hair first. I've never seen such a greasy head in all my life.'"

Now I will tell you three things: first, he never had that problem again; second, he got filled with the Spirit; and, third, he became my best friend.

But I have missed out the most important part— before I went to go and do that for him, I went alone into the church, I knelt down in my own pulpit and I tried to pray for James. Have you ever tried to pray for a sick man when you want him to stay sick? It's not easy. I struggled to pray for him and said, "Lord I don't want him to get better." Then, to my astonishment, I found myself praying for James with all my heart and soul, only I wasn't praying in English. It sounded a bit like Chinese, but I prayed for an hour in that language.

I remember looking at my watch and thinking, "I haven't been praying an hour? Yes! I wonder if I can do that again." I began to pray again in what sounded like Russian, and I was praying with all my heart and soul for James. That is when I understood Acts 2; that is when I knew what it was to receive the Holy Spirit – to be baptised in the Holy Spirit. Now I found myself doing things that I had never done before in my life. I found I could heal people; I found I could give them words of wisdom and knowledge; I found I could prophesy. A whole new world opened up.

That's the new covenant and that's being baptised in the Holy Spirit. I am so glad it happened to me when I was on my own, and then I wasn't thinking it was somebody else doing it for me – except Jesus.

But that's only the beginning; that's only a one-off experience. To *go on* being filled—that's the secret, because we leak. We need to go on being filled up with the Holy Spirit. All that makes the new covenant real.

The Spirit is writing the laws of God on your heart. The Spirit is softening your heart of stone. The Spirit is conveying God's forgiveness to you and giving you a clean conscience—what a gift that is. Well that's the new covenant that was achieved in the New Testament by our Lord Jesus Christ and his Holy Spirit. Christ working *for* us, the Holy Spirit working *in* us – that is the new covenant and it is the best covenant in the whole Bible.

That puts you in a *new covenant people*. Even though it happens to you as an individual, now you feel what is called the fellowship of the Spirit with all kinds of people. People you might never have been friends with at all – now you recognise the same Holy Spirit in them as in you. Whatever their personality whatever their race, whatever their background—you recognise the *same* Holy Spirit, and you know that the Spirit who is in me is in him, in her, and therefore you find the fellowship of the Holy Spirit who binds you together in a new fellowship in a new body, the body of Christ, his flock, his family.

THE OTHER COVENANTS – continued

Note pattern   – international and national

NOAHIC   – Matt. 5:45b

ABRAHAMIC – Luke 1:54, 72

Matt. 22:32

Heb. 6:13–20

DAVIDIC   – Luke 1:32; Acts 13:34; Rom. 1:3;

John 7:42; Acts 15:16;

"Son of David" – Mark 11:10; Matt. 12:23;

21:9, 15; 22:42; Rev 3:7; 5:5; 22:16

THE "OLD" COVENANT – cancelled

MOSAIC   'old' – Heb. 8:6

obsolete – Heb. 8:13

versus Mosaic – John 1:17; Rom.10:4–11;

Gal. 4:21–31

dead to law – Rom. 7:4

temporary – Gal 3:23–25

8

What about the others?

So what happens to those other covenants, now that we have a new covenant? Far too many Christians think that the new covenant stands alone and all the others have been left behind and can be forgotten—far from it. Let's run through them again.

As we have seen, the *Noahic* covenant is still in operation. It was made with the *whole human race* and it was God's promise to keep the seasons going and to ensure that the human race will always have enough food to eat, by supplying the light and moisture that produces all our food. So God has kept the covenant of Noah, and Jesus himself referred to it in the Sermon on the Mount when he said, "God sends his sun on the good and the evil. He sends his rain on the just and the unjust" (Matthew 5:45). God gave an *unconditional* covenant to Noah that he would keep the seasons going and keep the human race supplied with food, and he has kept that covenant.

What about the *Abrahamic* covenant? Well, as we have seen, even the New Testament, in the letter to the Hebrews (6:13–18), emphasises that when God made a covenant with Abraham, he swore an oath that he would keep it. God can't say, "By God, I'll keep my word," but he can say, "By myself I swear." God did that with Abraham. Furthermore he sealed it with blood and they killed an animal and God and Abraham walked between the halves of the animal together — that's a very serious covenant.

"Therefore," says the letter to the Hebrews in the New Testament, "God's covenant with Abraham still operates and still stands." The main thing that covenant included for Abraham and his descendants was the Promised Land, in the Middle East. Therefore I am among those who believe sincerely and by conviction that the major factor in the Middle East is that God gave that land to the Jewish people for ever but the politicians will not take any notice of that. They discuss every other issue except God's gift in the Middle East situation.

So the Abrahamic covenant still stands and, when Jesus was born, Mary rejoiced that God had remembered his covenant with Abraham. She recognised that when Jesus came, he came to endorse the Abrahamic covenant (see Luke 1:54f, 72f; Matthew 22:32; Hebrews 6:13–20).

What about the *Davidic covenant* now – the promise that one day a son of David would sit on the throne? Earlier, I mentioned the two rings I wear, both inscribed with the name David in Hebrew. This reminds me of the Davidic covenant whereby God promised that one day a son of David would sit on the throne of Israel forever. We know who that is. I am looking forward to the day when Jesus restores the kingdom to Israel and sits on David's throne. It is going to happen because God said it would (see Luke 1:32f; Acts 13:34; Romans 1:3; John 7:42; Acts 15:16).

So those covenants are still operating; they are still valid; they can still be trusted. But there is one covenant which doesn't operate for Christians, and that is *the covenant of Moses*. It includes the law of Moses which is not one but 613 laws and you can find them in the books of Exodus, Leviticus and Deuteronomy. If we were still under that covenant we would all have to keep all those laws. I have not yet met a Jew who manages to keep them all, never mind a Gentile.

Not to keep them all is to be under God's curse. Earlier, we thought about why the Jews have been blessed more than any other nation and cursed more than any other nation. God has kept his promise to bless them if they kept the law or to curse them if they didn't. ***That's the Mosaic Law but we are not under*** *that law any more.* It really is a relief to me to know that the old covenant has been replaced by the new one, and that Mosaic law has dropped out (see John 1:17; Romans 7:4; 10:4–11; Galatians 3:23–25; 4:21–31; Hebrews 8:6, 13).

At this point it will be helpful to recall the Council that met in Jerusalem to decide what to do about the first major controversy in the early church (read all about it in Acts 15). The issue was about circumcision, but behind that was the question whether Gentiles who had been brought to faith in Jesus, the Jewish Messiah (in Greek 'Christ'), should become Jewish themselves, by being circumcised (the men only, of course).

Paul fought vehemently against this notion, primarily on the grounds that that would bind them to keep the whole of the Mosaic legislation (Galatians 5:3). God wants to save Gentiles without bringing them into such bondage, much less the curse on those who fail to be totally obedient. Peter came to Paul's aid by reporting God's acceptance of Cornelius. James, the Lord's brother, who chaired the debate, summed it up by releasing Gentiles from any such burdens and drafted a letter asking them to consider the sensitive scruples of any Jewish members in their fellowships.

Since then churches have been reluctant to apply this ruling consistently. Some Christian scholars have divided the Mosaic legislation into different categories – ceremonial, civil and moral, for example – ignoring the fact they are not so split up in the original text but clearly presented as an integrated whole. They then claim that the moral requirements still apply, while conveniently ignoring the attached sanctions (particularly the death sentence for over a dozen lapses, e.g. adultery).

This explains why the Ten Commandments have appeared on the walls and windows of many church buildings and been recited in their liturgies. But there have been more serious vestiges of the Mosaic covenant in church life.

One of the most damaging is the perpetuated division between priests and people, enshrined in the architecture of the tabernacle tent and later temple. The distinction between professional 'clergy' and amateur 'laity' and the transition from one to the other by ordination has blighted many, if not most, church structures. The Reformers rediscovered the priesthood of all believers but did not apply it consistently to their ministry.

Another was to try and establish the theocracy of Israel, which was both a political and a religious entity, hence its mixture of civic and ceremonial laws. This has led to confusion in Church/State relations, with Church States (from Geneva to Rome) and State Churches (established by law), both of which are disintegrating today.

The baptism of babies is justified by appeal to the 'old' covenant which included the children of parents already within it, confirmed by circumcision. This was reinforced by State Churches, which could hardly refuse baptism of the offspring of good citizens.

The sabbath (Saturday) was changed to Sunday (the day of resurrection) by the Church's own authority, but still regarded as fulfilling the fourth commandment, a holy day of rest. Some church bodies still insist on Saturday observance, like the Seventh Day Adventists and the Congregation of Jahweh. In the same way, the Church kept the main Jewish festivals (Passover, Pentecost and Tabernacles) but changed the dating of the first two from the moon to the sun calendar and ignored the third altogether, transferring the birth of Jesus to the pagan midwinter feast which became Christmas.

For obvious reasons, many churches retained the Mosaic requirement to give a tenth (or tithe) of one's income to the authorities. Surviving tithe barns testify to the days when it was paid in kind. Surprisingly, many recently formed fellowships have made it a condition of membership, thus assuring stable income. But a tenth may be too much for some believers (single mothers?)

and too little for many. The New Testament has replaced this Jewish tax with giving – sacrificial, regular, generous, proportionate and voluntary ('cheerful' means the Lord only wants what we want to give; but he notes what we keep!).

With most advocates of applying the Mosaic law to Christians there seems to be a 'pick 'n' mix' attitude, a highly subjective selection of which can be transferred to the 'new' covenant. Actually, scripture itself repeats some of the old laws and these must be accepted by believers. For example, nine of the ten commandments are thus endorsed (not the fourth; see Romans 14:5–8; Colossians 2:16). Indeed, some of them are defined in even stricter terms. 'Thou shalt not murder' forbids contempt and hatred; 'Thou shalt not commit adultery' includes lusting looks and even remarriage after divorce (Matthew 5:21–32).

In fact there are *more* imperative commands in the 'new' covenant than the 'old' (over 1100 compared to over 600)! The Christian may not be 'under the law' of Moses but that does not mean that he/she is under no law at all. This is the heresy of 'antinomianism' (from 'anti' = against and 'nomos' = law in Greek). Such heretics claim that we only need the presence and guidance of the Holy Spirit to keep all God's laws or that the love he has shed abroad in our hearts will fulfil the law. This has led to the 'situational ethics' in which love is the only absolute principle. An over-emphasis on grace is another characteristic.

What do we say to such arguments? First, it is a criticism of the Holy Spirit, who inspired so much ethical exhortation in the New Testament (what a waste of paper!). Second, it is a criticism of Jesus himself, who commanded his apostles to make disciples by teaching them 'to obey everything I have commanded you' (Matthew 28:20). Thirdly, and most significantly, it denies the continuing influence of the 'old man', the flesh, after having become a 'new man', the spirit. Habits and memories can still draw one back into the former lifestyle. This explains the paradox of New Testament teaching. The old man is dead but won't lie down, so kill him off. Put off the old lifestyle and put on the new, because you have been crucified with Christ and raised with him to newness of life. The moral appeal can be summed up as: 'Become what you already are'.

Jesus and his apostles were convinced that their 'disciples' would need clear commandments to live by. Hence the need to follow up preaching (what God has done for us) with teaching (what we should do for him). It can be called 'the law of Christ' and 'the royal law'. Both titles distinguish it from the law of Moses. There is a different motive ('If you obey my commands, you will remain in my love; John 15:10). Above all, the new covenant offers both the power and the desire to obey. So it is also called: 'the law of liberty'.

To put all this another way, there are plenty of laws to bother with in the new covenant without adding a few hundred more from the old! Either is formidable enough without the other. There is a comic yet tragic book by an American, agnostic, Jewish journalist who tried to keep both for just twelve months (*The Year of Living Biblically* by A J Jacobs, published by Arrow books). His efforts were thorough and utterly sincere. Significantly he found the 'new' imperatives harder than the 'old' and never discovered the secret (salvation) of the former, eventually giving up as 'a reverent agnostic'. All who try to keep the divine laws in their own strength should read his hilarious misadventures, enough to put you off for life!

Finally, there are two further recent trends that require comment, both related to the re-establishment of the State of Israel in 1948, namely the resurging numbers of Christian Zionists and Messianic Jews.

Christians who were convinced that God would fulfil his promise to bring the Jews back to their own land played a significant role in their return, from the middle of the eighteenth century. There were not many, most of them in the Church of England. Since their re-appearance on the political map, the number of sympathetic supporters in the world-wide Church has increased to millions, represented by thousands attending the annual celebration of the Feast of Tabernacles, organised by the International Christian Embassy. However, some of these welcome friends of Israel have allowed their newly discovered love for the nation to become an obsession. They seem to have forgotten that God loves Gentiles as Gentiles and that the early church was correct in refusing to insist that they become Jewish in order to belong to God's people. So they behave more and more as if they are not Gentiles but Jews, lighting candles on Friday evening, singing Hebrew songs of praise on Saturday morning with Israeli music and dancing, above all keeping (religiously) the annual Feasts described in the Torah, particularly Leviticus. So far they have drawn the line at adopting circumcision! But who knows where it will all end?

It is possible that they sincerely believe that they are helping to build that 'one new man' in Christ Jesus. But some of their antics rightly attract the ridicule and even contempt of sceptical Jews. More seriously, they are driving a wedge into the Gentile branch of God's family, even shutting themselves off from it. Above all, they are in danger of donning the mantle of the Judaizers who did so much to undermine Paul's missionary endeavours.

Paul was certainly willing to adopt Jewish behaviour in order to evangelise his fellow-Jews, even to the point of circumcising his colleague Timothy, but he jealously guarded his Gentile converts from becoming Jewish for any other reason (which he called 'another gospel'). He knew how dangerous that could be, having known the Mosaic covenant from the inside. He knew that in itself the law was 'holy, righteous and good' because of the God who made it for his people, but for Gentiles it was only bad news.

Which brings us to the second group, the Messianic Jews. There has always been a 'faithful remnant', right through the two thousand years of church history. But the number has been small and pressure has been put on them to renounce their Jewish roots and become Gentile 'Christians' (a word coined to describe Gentile believers in the Jewish Messiah). Since 1948 there has been an amazing increase in Jewish believers (variously labelled 'true', 'complete' or, mostly, 'Messianic' Jews), both in the nation and among those Jews still scattered among the other nations (about 50%). The total at the time of writing is estimated at about 50,000, with about 15,000 of these in Israel itself. The growing number of such individuals has made possible the emergence of corporate fellowships meeting together locally. For the first time since the first century A.D. there are now messianic assemblies or 'Jewish churches'. This is the great new fact in the ecumenical scene, but traditional denominations are taking their time to realise it. The major question facing such groups is how much of the Torah to include in their constitution and discipline (by 'Torah' they mean the first five books of the Bible, though only four cover the Mosaic law). This is the major issue in their debates and there is a wide spectrum of opinion among them, which could threaten their unity. Should their main worship services be on a Saturday (most agree)? Should their membership be limited to ethnic Jews (some agree)? Should Hebrew be their exclusive language (a few agree, but assemblies in the Diaspora usually use additional indigenous tongues)?

Perhaps the most important thing to say is that their eternal salvation is in no way affected by how much or how little of the law of Moses is kept. The new covenant, which was originally intended for them, was also designed to *replace* the covenant made with Moses at Sinai (Jeremiah 31:30–32). There is even a danger of observing the law of Moses at all if it is thought that this will establish a righteousness before God which is an adequate substitute for the divine righteousness offered through the Messiah (Romans 10:1–13).

In other words, whether a believing Jew keeps any, some or all of the Mosaic legislation is entirely a matter of personal preference, a voluntary choice. However, there are sound reasons for retaining much of Jewish culture after coming to faith, mainly to keep relationships with family, friends and associates, not least in the hope of helping them to share in the true liberty of the new covenant, the freedom not to sin. This is to identify for the sake of evangelism.

There has therefore been a profound reversal since the days of the Jerusalem Council (in Acts 15). Then the issue was whether to accept Gentile believers without their becoming like Jews. Now the church has to decide whether to accept Jewish believers without their becoming like Gentiles! And there are many remaining practical questions about the relationships between Gentile and Jewish churches: How do they demonstrate their unity in Christ (Messiah)? By interchangeable ministry and membership?

The question of circumcision takes on a new dimension. Should Messianic believers circumcise their baby boys? Would that obligate them to keep the whole 'law', as Paul said it would Gentiles?

The first thing to point out is that circumcision was part of the Abrahamic covenant (Genesis 17:10–14), not the Mosaic. And, as we have seen, this covenant is endorsed by and continued alongside the new covenant.

Therefore circumcision of a Jewish boy identifies him as a physical descendant of Abraham (Gentile Christians are only spiritual descendants, sharing his faith but not his flesh). He is, by the same token, entitled to the physical blessings promised to the multiple seed (offspring) of the patriarch, primarily the 'land' in the Middle East, its boundaries clearly defined by God himself, its ultimate owner and landlord (Genesis 15:18–21).

Jesus himself believed that the ethnic identity of the nation of Israel would persist until the earth itself disappeared, as the prophet Jeremiah had predicted (Jeremiah 31:35–36, the same chapter in which the new covenant was announced for *them*). He promised the twelve apostles that they would sit on twelve thrones judging the twelve tribes of Israel (Matthew 19:28; Luke 22:30). To those who believe that Jesus is returning to rule the nations, both his own and all the others, this promise clearly relates to the millennial kingdom preceding the demise of this present earth (the 'pre-millennial' view of his second advent). Incidentally, this assurance of future responsibility means that there are no 'lost' tribes to the Lord.

Beyond that will be the consummation of one flock

under one shepherd in one fold (John 10:16). For all eternity one new man will live in one new heaven and earth with one new capital city – albeit with a Jewish name (Jerusalem) and twenty-four Jewish names inscribed on its gates (the twelve tribes) and foundations (the twelve apostles), representing the whole biblical history of God's people. And God himself will change his address from heaven to earth and to angelic astonishment live with human beings (Revelation 21:3). After all, this was his objective behind every covenant he ever made.

Other books by David Pawson

Come with me through Galatians
Come with me through Isaiah
Come with me through John
Come with me through Jude
Come with me through Mark
Come with me through Revelation
Christianity Explained
Defending Christian Zionism
The God and the Gospel of Righteousness
Is John 3:16 the Gospel?
Israel in the New Testament
Jesus: The Seven Wonders of HIStory
Jesus Baptises in One Holy Spirit
Leadership is Male
Living in Hope
Not As Bad As The Truth (autobiography)
Once Saved, Always Saved?
Practising the Principles of Prayer
The Challenge of Islam to Christians
The Normal Christian Birth
Remarriage is Adultery Unless...
The Road to Hell
Unlocking the Bible
When Jesus Returns
Where has the Body been for 2000 years? (Church history for beginners)
Why Does God Allow Natural Disasters?
Word and Spirit Together

Books by David Pawson are available in the USA from
www.pawsonbooks.com

Unlocking the Bible
is also available in DVD format from
www.davidpawson.com
Video on demand: www.christfaithmedia.com

Ebooks
Most books by David Pawson are also available as ebooks
amazon.com and amazon.co.uk

For details of foreign language editions and a full listing of
David Pawson Teaching Catalogue in MP3/DVD
or to purchase David Pawson books in the UK
please visit: www.davidpawson.com
Email: info@davidpawsonministry.com

Chinese language books by David Pawson
www.bolbookstore.com *and* www.elimbookstore.com.tw